THE HANDYMAN DICTIONARY

A Guide for the Home Mess-It-Up-Yourselfer

Illustrated by Janet Cleland

Published in the United States of America
by Hallmark Cards, Inc.

ISBN: 0-87529-661-0

Library of Congress Catalog Number: 92-73783

Printed in the United States of America.

ALLEN WRENCH: The wrench you loaned to your next-door neighbor Allen six months ago and haven't seen since.

APPETITE: What a guy builds up tightening a screw.

APPRECIATION: A feeling most women lack when it comes to a $450 ratchet set in a convenient plastic carrying case.

AWL: 1) A sharp, pointed tool used for poking holes in wood or leather. 2) Word often used in workshops throughout the South, as in, "Hand me that can of motah awl..."

BALL PEEN HAMMER: A small, round-headed hammer you're forced to drive nails with when one of the kids loses your regular hammer.

BARGAIN: Any tool used on more than one project.

BROKE: 1) In a state of disrepair. 2) Future condition of someone who buys a house labeled a "fixer-upper."

BZZZT!: Last sound you hear after the home handyman tries to replace a few fuses.

CAP: Crucial item in the handyman's wardrobe.

CAULK GUN: Common tool that causes the guy using it to unconsciously hum the theme from a spy movie and affect a firing pose.

CHUCK: 1) Part of the drill that holds the bit. 2) What the home handyman has to do to most of the projects he uses the drill on.

CLEANING: Activity a guy won't do for money in the house, but spends all afternoon doing in his beloved garage.

CORDLESS DRILL: A type of drill that won't mess up the reception on a workshop TV.
GO! GO! GO!
WWRRRRR

DECK: Wooden outdoor fun center which took many, many hours and dollars to build, which the family now stares at from inside the air-conditioned kitchen.

DIRECTIONS: Unnecessary and misleading written instructions which insult the intelligence of any true handyman.

DO-IT-YOURSELF: What a guy tells any family member who asks him to fix something during the big game.

DUD: Any nail that bends, no matter how incorrectly you may have hit it.

EARTH: Area in which you think you're the best handyman.

EASY: How you describe a home do-it-yourself project that will cost hundreds of dollars to have a professional repair the damage from later.

ELECTRIC HEDGE CLIPPERS: Modern lawn tool that produces uneven hedges in one-fourth the time of the old hand-operated variety.

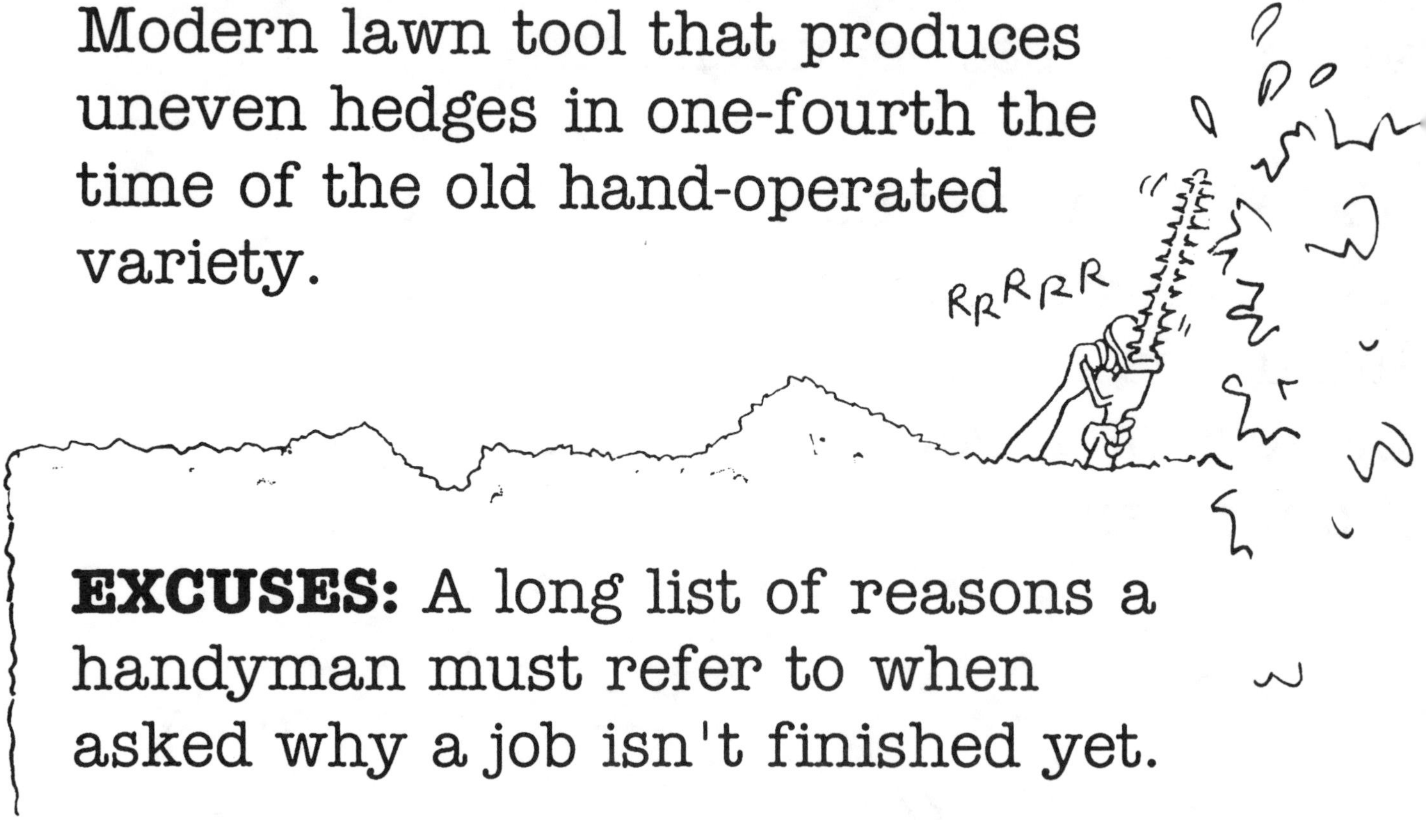

EXCUSES: A long list of reasons a handyman must refer to when asked why a job isn't finished yet.

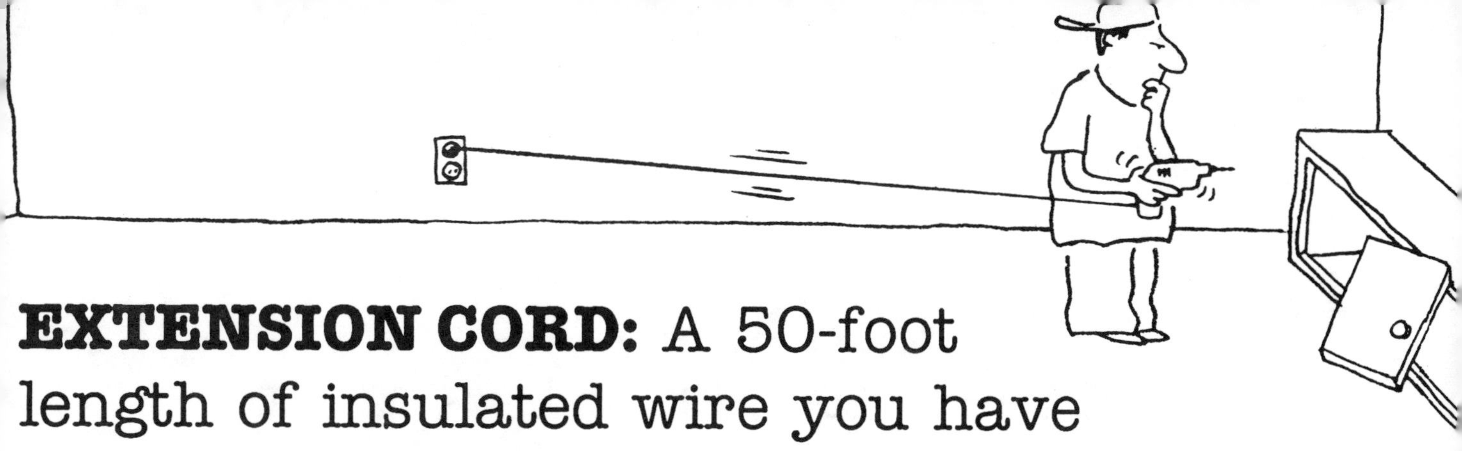

EXTENSION CORD: A 50-foot length of insulated wire you have to tear the garage apart to find because the cord on your drill is six inches too short.

"EYEBALL IT": How you miss most measurements by at least a foot.

FINISHED: An obvious misprint. No project is ever finished.

FLOAT: 1) A device used to maintain the water level in a toilet tank. 2) What the family seeks refuge on when the family handyman tries to fix a leaky sink.

FOOTBALL GAME: What you're in the middle of when the emergency that just has to be taken care of right now happens.

FRIEND: Someone who will lend you power tools.

FURNACE FILTER SCHEDULE: What you say you keep the calendar with the scantily-clad women on your garage wall to monitor.

GARAGE: A guy's second home. SEE ALSO: Secluded Retreat, Private Club and Vacation Cottage.

GARBAGE DISPOSAL: Something a guy has no interest in if it's time to clean up after dinner, but can't take apart fast enough if it's "making a funny noise."

GAS: What you run out of 10 minutes before dark with a quarter of the yard still to mow.

GREEN: The color of the neighbor's lawn.

HARDWARE STORE: See also: Paradise.

HEAVEN: A home workshop with cable.

HOT TUB: A large receptacle full of relaxing, bubbling hot water, which the wife is sure you should be able to install in a half-bath.

HOW-TO BOOKS: A series of home improvement guides purchased for the man of the house one Christmas, which have remained unopened on his workshop shelf ever since.

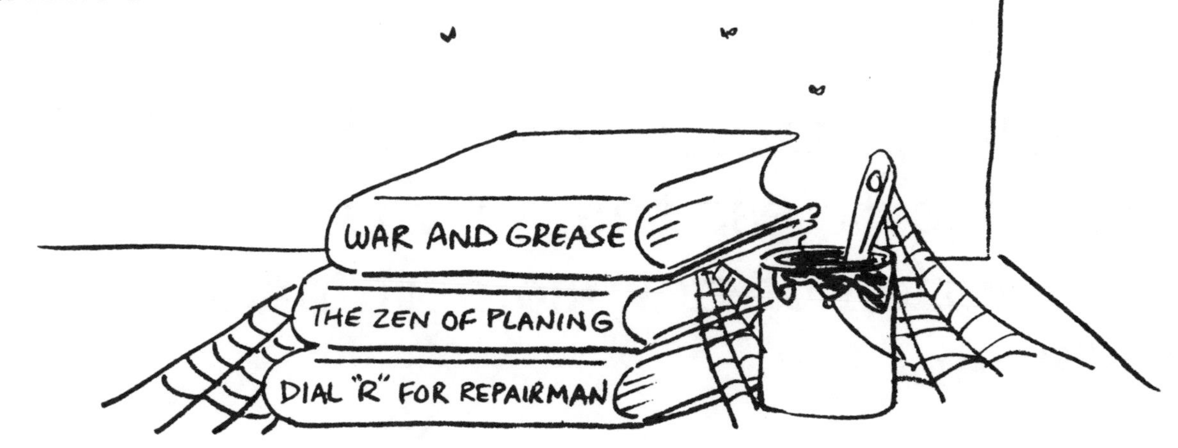

I-BEAM: How you feel when you actually finish a project.

ILLUSTRATION: The one thing more worthless than a written description of how something goes together.

INCH: The unit of measure you were off for the entire project.

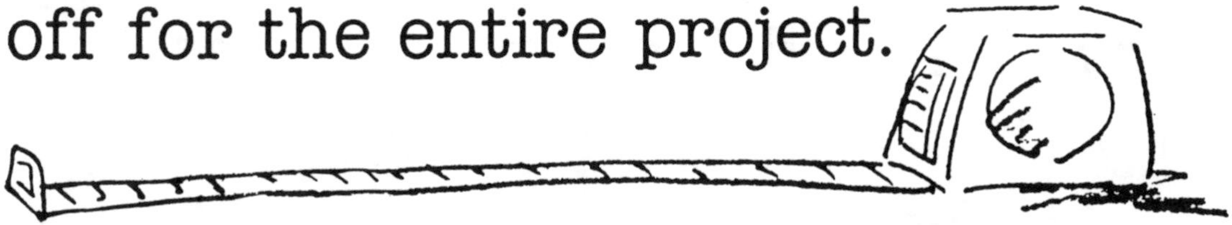

INSULATION: Something you take out a home improvement loan to buy in bulk quantities because you thought you saw a tiny shaft of light through a hairline crack in the attic.

JACKET: An article of clothing you wear in the shop which you narrowly saved from being thrown out by the wife just because of a couple of holes in the elbows, fraying around the collar, a broken zipper and some permanent stains.

JAGGED: The edge of pretty much anything you pick up when you're trying to fix something in a hurry.

JUICE: Handyman slang for electrical power. But its most common usage is: "I'm sweatin' like a pig in here! Go get me some juice!"

JUNK: The wife's description of anything to emerge from your workshop.

KARATE: 1) An oriental form of self-defense involving kicks and punches. 2) A good way to start a lawn mower.

KEY: Something you lost, making it impossible to get into your brand- new $500 stainless steel tool storage unit.

KIDS: Small people whose job it is to make sure Dad always has plenty of things to repair around the house.

KING: A guy on his riding lawn mower.

KISS OF DEATH: What your project has been given when your brother-in-law asks if he can help.

LADDER: What the wife needs to reach the new cabinets you installed in the kitchen.

LEGEND: A little nickname you've given yourself around the workshop.

LEGS: What you shorten a half inch, one at a time to stop the coffee table you built from rocking, until it reaches a height of about 5 inches.

LEVEL: An instrument used by the home do-it-yourselfer to determine that whatever he built isn't.

MECHANIC: A man who lives to make you feel small.

MIRACLE: An unusual event, such as a kid actually putting a tool back in the proper place.

MOVE: What your wife decided she wants to do after you've got the house looking perfect.

MUD: 1) Plaster used while hanging drywall. 2) The name given to anybody who uses your tools without asking.

NAKED: The way you feel without a tool belt.

NECESSARY: What a handyman calls pretty much every tool ever invented.

NEIGHBORHOOD: Area where you have to borrow a neighbor's power tool because another neighbor already borrowed yours.

"**NOT A TOY**": Phrase used to describe any new tool to the kids.

NUMBSKULL: What you get after a board from the brand-new tree house falls on your head.

OIL CHANGE: Something you spend big money on special wrenches, ramps, rags and clothing to do yourself, thereby making a huge slippery mess of the garage and the driveway, but saving the 13 bucks you would have paid a professional to do it in 30 minutes or less.

ORANGE: Color of the extension cord the wife doesn't want you to buy because it clashes with the decor.

OUT: Where your back goes once you're wedged behind the washing machine looking for the leak.

PEG-BOARD: Durable brown paneling with holes in it, more prized for workshop walls than marble, stained glass or painted velvet.

PENICILLIN: What is growing in the coffee cup that's been sitting on your workbench since last winter.

PINE: 1) An attractive, durable wood, used for carpentry. 2) What a handyman does at the biggest power tool sale of the year.

PING!: The sound the car was making before you fixed it so it will make no sound at all. Ever.

POWER SURGE: The wave of confidence that makes a beginner think that shiny new tools are an adequate substitute for know-how.

QUAKE: What the house does every time the furnace comes on since you made a few "minor adjustments."

QUART: Amount of transmission fluid left on the driveway after you fixed that leaking transmission.

QUINTESSENTIAL: That moment you open a brand new tool box.

QUIVER: What guys do at the mere thought of buying a new power tool.

RABBIT EARS: Antique television attachment that delivers a snowy, rolling picture that a handyman swears is "as good as cable."

RACHET: Actually, a pretty funny word, when you think about it.

REFUND: What you ask for when you take in a tool because it's defective, then find out you've been using it wrong.

RIGHT ARM: What most home handymen would give to have their own how-to show.

SAW: What you use to cut sawhorses in two.

SHOP: 1) What a guy hates to do. 2) If preceded by "wood" or "auto," where a guy loves to be.

SHOP VAC: The only cleaning equipment a guy will cheerfully use, probably because of its resemblance to a cool robot!

SOCKET WRENCH: What the handyman experiences in his shoulder when the hand-held power saw is faster than he is.

"SSSSHHHHYYAH-OW!": What a guy says in front of the kids when he pinches that skin between his finger and thumb with the needle-nose pliers.

TAPE MEASURE: A crutch for the novice handyman who hasn't learned to "eyeball it."

TELEVISION: Fuzzy-pictured, paint-spotted, small-screen garage appliance that has no knobs and must be turned on with pliers and is permanently tuned to the all-sports network.

TOOL BELT: A garage wall's worth of tools that some genius decided he wanted to wear, and it caught on.

TURPENTINE: Liquid hand soap for guys.

UNDERWATER: Where a guy is by the time he gets the toilet unclogged.

UNDERWEAR: What every cleaning rag in your shop is made of.

USELESS: Any tool made by a manufacturer that isn't the handyman's personal favorite.

VARNISH: Sticky, fume-laden liquid applied to unfinished wood to give tiny airborne sawdust particles a place to embed themselves.

VAULTED CEILING: What the handyman did when the dog knocked over his ladder.

VISCOSITY: Adjective commonly used to describe motor oil even though nobody has the slightest idea what the heck it means.

VISE: Four-hundred pound, steel-forged, 8,000 psi torque implement you have to reinforce the floor to support, which you use mostly for cracking walnuts at Christmas.

WAIST: Part of the body a true handyman's belt hangs well below.

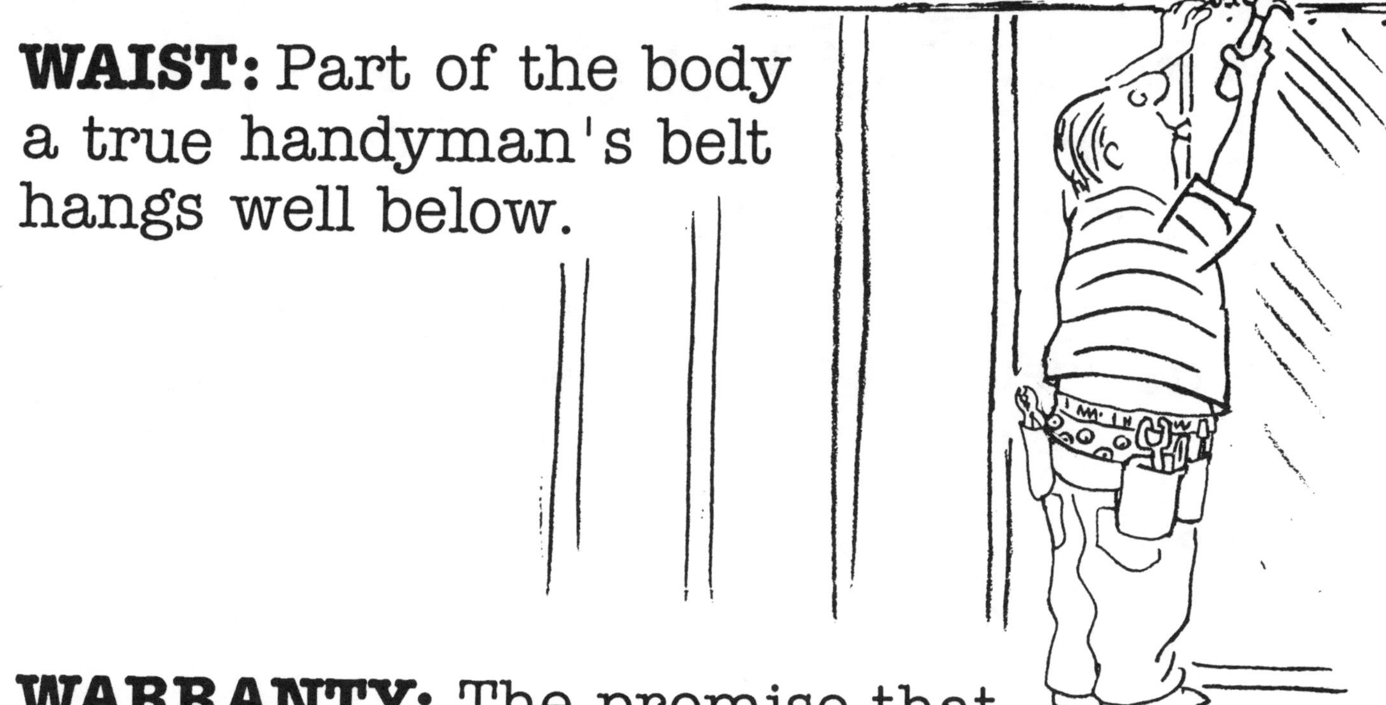

WARRANTY: The promise that expires just before your power tool does.

"**WHAT ABOUT NOW?**": What a guy yells from the roof as he tries to adjust the antenna to get something besides snow on the TV he decided not to buy cable for so he could "save hundreds in costly bills."

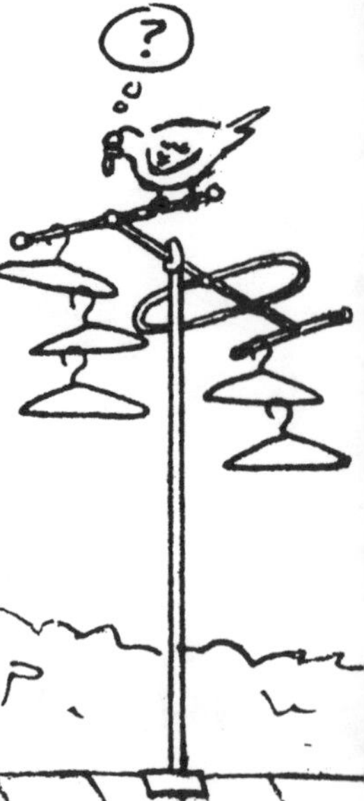

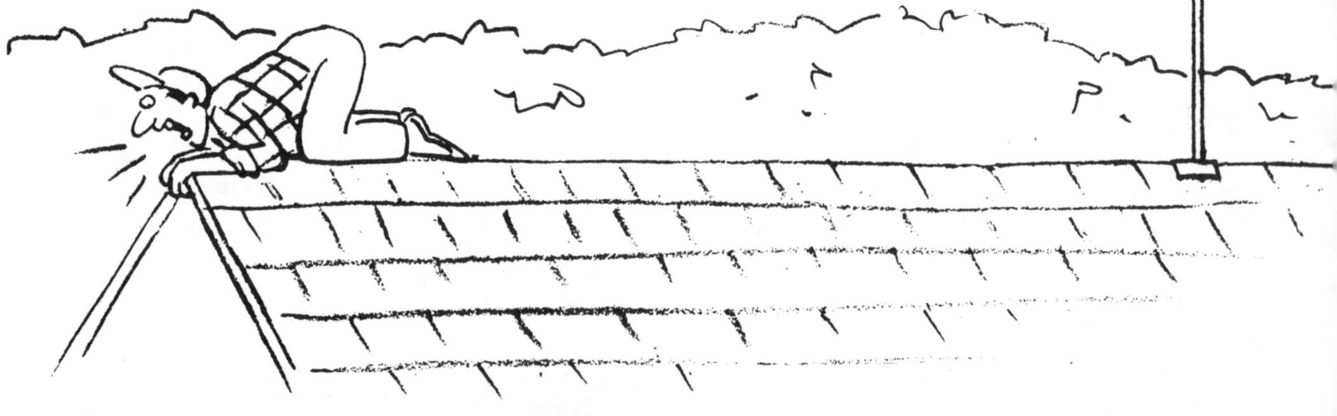

WIGGLE: What kids will do with any tool you ask them to hold very still.

WINDOW: A do-it-yourself project that started out as a front door security peephole, and just kind of got out of control.

"X-IE" ONE: How Mom and the kids describe a Phillips head screwdriver.

X-RAY: How the doctor locates the roofing nails you were holding in your mouth when the ladder slipped.

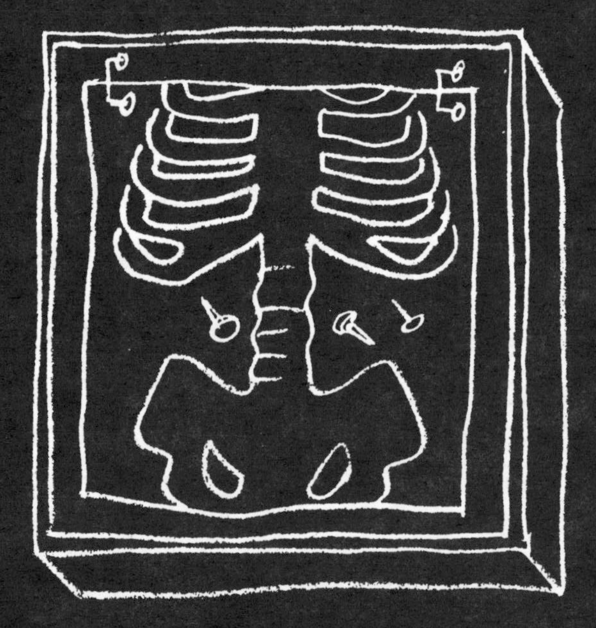

YACHT: The ultimate build-in-your-basement project, often left half-finished when the handyman realizes there's no way to get it out of the basement.

Y-CONNECTOR: A device which allows water to leak through two pipes instead of one.

YEAR: Length of time it takes most home handymen to complete a two-week project.

YELLOW CAB: Who you call for transportation after doing a minor tune-up on the family car.

ZERO: The amount of patience the handyman has for assembly instructions.

ZIGZAG: The pattern you get when you try to saw with a bumblebee in the room.

"**ZZZZZZZZ**": 1) The sound made by a power saw as it cuts through a board. 2) The sound made by a home handyman, minutes after he finishes anything as strenuous as sawing through a board.

WRITTEN BY: Chris Brethwaite, Bill Bridgeman, Bill Gray, Allyson Jones, Kevin Kinzer, Mark Oatman, Dee Ann Stewart, Dan Taylor, Rich Warwick and Myra Zirkle.

Books from:

SHOEBOX GREETINGS

(A tiny little division of Hallmark)

STILL MARRIED AFTER ALL THESE YEARS
DON'T WORRY, BE CRABBY: Maxine's Guide to Life
40: THE YEAR OF NAPPING DANGEROUSLY
THE MOM DICTIONARY
THE DAD DICTIONARY
WORKIN' NOON TO FIVE: The Official Workplace Quiz Book
WHAT... ME, 30?
THE FISHING DICTIONARY
YOU EXPECT ME TO SWALLOW THAT? The Official Hospital Quiz Book
THE GOOD, THE PLAID AND THE BOGEY: A Glossary of Golfing Terms
THE CHINA PATTERN SYNDROME: Your Wedding and How to Survive It
THE GRANDPARENT DICTIONARY
STILL A BABE AFTER ALL THESE YEARS?
CRABBY ROAD: More Thoughts on Life From Maxine
THE HANDYMAN DICTIONARY A Guide For the Home Mess-It-Up-Yourselfer